# Homes in the Future

**Mark Lambert**

Lerner Publications Company
Minneapolis

All words printed in **bold** are explained
in the glossary on page 30.

Cover illustration *These experimental homes in New
Mexico U.S.A. were built with the idea of using as little
utility service as possible.*

First published in the U.S. in 1989 by
Lerner Publications Company.

First published 1988 by Wayland (Publishers) Ltd.

**Library of Congress Cataloging-in-Publication Data**

Lambert, Mark, 1946-
    Homes in the future.

    Bibliography: p.
    Includes index.
    Summary: Discusses aspects of homes of the future,
including their design, sources of energy, and security systems.
    1. Dwellings—Forecasting—Juvenile literature.
[1. Dwellings—Forecasting] I. Title.
NA7120.L36   1989              643'.1              88-9390
ISBN 0-8225-2126-1 (lib. bdg.)

Printed in Italy by G. Canale & C. S.p.A. - Turin
Bound in the United States of America

1  2  3  4  5  6  7  8  9  10  97  96  95  94  93  92  91  90  89  88

# Contents

# Past, present, and future

For most of us, home is an essential part of our lives. It is a private place where we can rest from work, eat our food, and keep the things that belong to us. The first homes were the caves and tents used by our early ancestors as they roamed about in search of food. About 10,000 years ago, people began to settle down and farm the land. They began to build their own dwellings using the materials they had available, such as stones, mud, and grass. Later, such materials were replaced by wood cut from trees and bricks made of clay.

*Above*   In Britain 3,000 years ago, during the Bronze Age, homes were built of crude timbers and thatched with straw.

*Left*   Today's homes in a modern city such as Sydney, Australia, are built of brick and concrete.

*Right*   In the distant future, colonies of people may live in huge spinning cylinders in space. Using energy from the sun, they will be able to be independent of earth.

While most houses are still built using traditional methods and materials, in recent years other materials have become available. These materials, together with new building techniques, have led to some interesting ideas for homes in the future. At the same time, people have become much more aware of the need to conserve energy by reducing the amount used in homes. Future homes will have to be designed to reduce heat loss.

As the world's population has increased, so has the need for many more homes. Villages have grown into towns, and towns into cities. At present, there is still plenty of room on earth, but in the distant future, the world may begin to run out of available land on which to build. Perhaps by that time, humans may be starting to colonize space. People may be living in huge specially built colonies that orbit the sun like miniature planets.

# Cities and towns of the future

Most of the world's 5,100 million people live in towns and cities. This is largely a result of the **Industrial Revolution** of the 1700s and 1800s, when people began to move to the cities in order to find work. Today, city people have become used to living in relatively close contact with others, and most now seem to prefer it.

But the populations of most towns and cities are constantly increasing. Experts estimate that by the year 2000 there will be 6,200 million people in the world and that this figure will have increased to 10,000 million by the year 2100. Cities will therefore grow in size, and city planners will have to decide whether cities should be made to grow upwards or outwards.

*Right*   *In this design for a 2,150-foot-(650-meter-) high building, the modules, each containing office space and living space, are assembled around a central core. The network of cables gives the building strength and prevents it from swaying too much.*

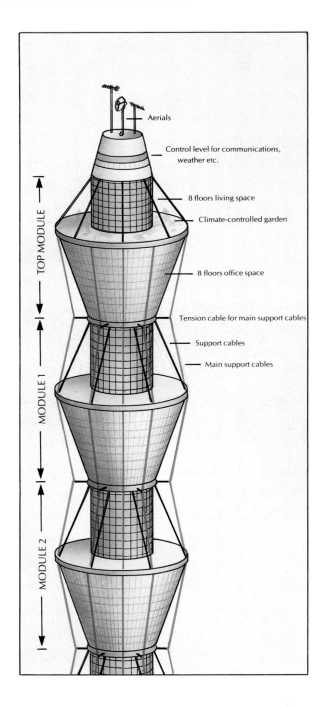

Aerials

Control level for communications, weather etc.

8 floors living space

Climate-controlled garden

8 floors office space

Tension cable for main support cables

Support cables

Main support cables

TOP MODULE

MODULE 1

MODULE 2

*In the past, designers thought that building tall (high-rise) blocks of apartments was the best way of providing homes. Using this rule, they hoped to prevent cities from spreading too much and taking over land that was needed for farming. However, such massive towers are very expensive to build and maintain properly. Due partly to neglect and partly to poor building materials, many high-rise apartments have fallen into disrepair. The best alternative seems to be to build imaginatively designed, "low-rise" blocks in towns and cities. No more than three or four stories high, these low-rises would provide yards and other outside areas for the inhabitants.*

**Above**   *Huge skyscrapers may look spectacular, but will the average person want to live in such buildings?*

**Right**   *Low-rise apartment blocks can be pleasant to live in, but they may use up valuable land area.*

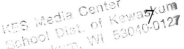

# Designing future homes

Modern high technology, based on computers and information systems, has had considerable influence on what designers think future homes may be like. Many designs already use modern-looking materials, such as steel, glass, and plastics. Experts believe that computer technology —in addition to helping with the design itself—will play a large part in the running of future homes.

*Left* These homes in Montreal, Canada, have been fitted together in blocks to make a complex shape.

*Right* A house built into the ground, such as this one in Britain, conserves energy and blends into the landscape.

*Left* These high-tech houses in New Mexico are heated by the sun. The walls are made of a special insulating material.

However, all architects and house designers must take several things into account. First, and perhaps foremost, tomorrow's homes must be comfortable and pleasant to live in: no amount of computer gadgetry is going to make up for a house that is bare and uncomfortable. In addition, a house must be easy for people to live in. Everything must be in an appropriate place and space must be used sensibly. Finally, homes of the future must be as energy efficient as possible. They must be designed so that they use very little fuel and electricity, and they must be well insulated to prevent heat from escaping.

Designers have come up with a range of possible future homes. Domes, bubbles, and houses on legs have all been suggested. Another very interesting idea is that houses should be set into the ground, with most of the roof covered over by grass. Such houses would blend easily into the landscape and be very well insulated. However, they would be expensive to build.

# Building materials

Throughout history, people have built houses from the materials most easily available to them. Even today, most houses are built of stone, brick, and lumber. In recent years, house builders have used concrete blocks, which are made by using cement to bind together small pieces of gravel or other material.

It seems likely that builders will continue to use these materials. But two important factors will influence how future houses are built. Firstly, people will need to build houses that waste the least possible amount of energy. Secondly, the cost of building houses with traditional materials is increasing.

The outside walls of the most energy-efficient houses consist of two layers of bricks or other materials, with a cavity between them. To help insulate such houses, builders often use special insulation blocks —made of ash, **clinker**, or **silica**— to build the inner layer. The cavity can also be either lined or filled with a good insulating material.

**Left**  *Using pre-fabricated sections helps to reduce the cost of building homes.*

**Right**  *Well-insulated walls keep heat loss to a minimum. Here a timber frame is being covered with polystyrene foam, before being faced with bricks.*

*Above* Materials such as timber, concrete blocks, and bricks seem likely to remain popular for building homes for some time to come.

To reduce building costs, houses of the future may be built of well-insulated, **prefabricated** sections. The utility services—electricity, gas, and water—will probably still be installed in the traditional way. The careful use of tough, long-lasting materials will ensure that such houses do not need as much repair as today's houses. The actual layout and design of such future houses could be varied to suit each owner's taste. It is even possible to build houses with movable wall panels so the layout can be altered at any time the owners wish.

# Using suitable technology

In many parts of the world, people cannot afford to use the latest building materials. Yet their need for proper housing is no less than that of the inhabitants of more developed countries. People have become very skilled at using the available materials and the appropriate technology to build homes of a high standard. These homes make use of designs well adapted to local conditions.

In many hot countries, brick can be made from the local soil. New methods of producing better quality blocks will make houses quicker to build and stronger in the future.

Local soil can be turned into mud to form bricks. The bricks can be made resistant to wind and rain by adding cement or lime to the mud. Mud mixed with straw can be used to build houses that are warm in the winter and cool in the summer. Houses designed to allow natural air currents to flow through are especially cool in the summer, and they require no additional cooling equipment.

In cold countries, the main problem is to keep a home warm, particularly in the long winter months. Traditionally, the Lapps of northern

*Right* *In this Syrian village, a few concrete dwellings have been mixed with the traditional homes that were built using mud. Concrete is inappropriate here as it is very expensive. The traditional-style homes are also much cooler during the day.*

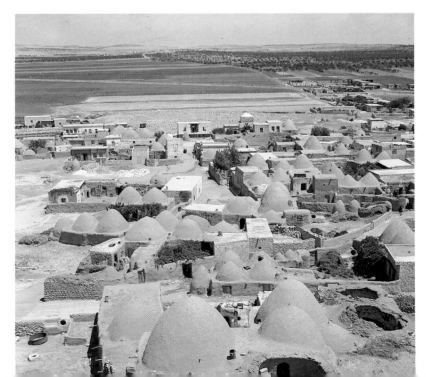

Europe and the Inuit of the Arctic were wandering peoples. The Inuit built dome-shaped igloos from blocks of snow. A dome-shaped house is ideal for cold climates because the smallest possible area is exposed to the outside. Modern Lapp and Inuit groups live in homes made largely of timber. Wood is a good insulator and can be very energy-efficient, particularly if homes are also insulated with a material such as fiberglass.

*Above    Traditional homes can sometimes be improved. Here a village in India is being reroofed with tiles made from local clay.*

*Right    The Inuit have adapted to living in modern, well-insulated, comfortable homes.*

13

# Energy for homes

The energy we use in today's homes comes from a variety of sources— electricity, coal, oil, natural gas, and wood. But as we use up these resources, so they are likely to become more scarce, and the way in which we use energy may become more controlled. Electricity is the cleanest form of energy that we use, but it has to be created by turning huge magnets, called rotors. These rotors spin past coils of wire, creating electricity. To turn the rotors, power plants usually burn **fossil fuels**, like oil, or use the heat produced by a nuclear reactor. These methods for producing electricity

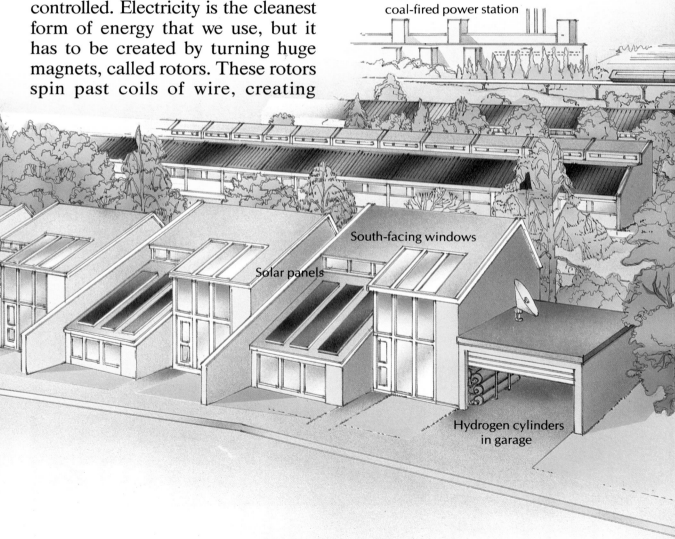

Medium-sized smoke-free coal-fired power station

South-facing windows

Solar panels

Hydrogen cylinders in garage

involve pollution and possible danger from radiation.

Nuclear power may be the main source of electricity in the future. On the other hand, it may become too unpopular and be abandoned.

*An energy-efficient town of the future will get its energy from a variety of sources.*

Windmills

Solar collectors

Battery car

Many people fear that nuclear power is too unpredictable and dangerous to rely on completely. Other energy sources that could be substituted include mountain rivers, the wind, tides, and waves. All of these forces could be used to turn the rotors that produce electricity without causing pollution or radiation. Also, geothermal power—producing electricity by using the heat from inside the earth—may eventually be commonplace.

Many homes will also have their own methods of producing energy. Solar panels, for example, are already used for collecting the sun's rays to produce hot water. Solar cells can convert sunlight directly into electricity. In some places, heat pumps are used to extract heat from the environment outside. Heat pumps can be used together with solar power. Solar power is used to produce warm water, which is then used by a heat pump to produce hot water.

# Conserving energy

Heat can enter or escape from a poorly insulated house very easily. A great deal of it passes through the walls or leaves the house through small gaps around badly fitting doors and windows. Some heat passes out through the relatively thin window glass and some rises up through the roof.

Many of these forms of heat loss can be overcome by taking fairly simple measures. The roofs, and where necessary the floors, of all houses should be lined with an insulating material, such as fiberglass or **vermiculite** chips. Doors and windows should be made draft-proof.

**Double-glazed** glass can be fitted to reduce heat loss through the windows. Any old windows that need replacing should be replaced with good quality double-glazed types.

In the future, houses will need to have all these features as standard. The walls of future houses will have to consist of, or at least include, materials that allow little or no heat to escape. If the south-facing wall is made of glass, this can help to trap the heat of the sun, thus saving other forms of energy that would be used to heat the house.

*Two vital ways of conserving energy in the home are insulating the roof space (**left**) and covering the hot water tank (**below**).*

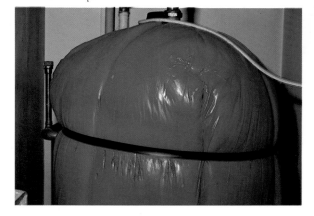

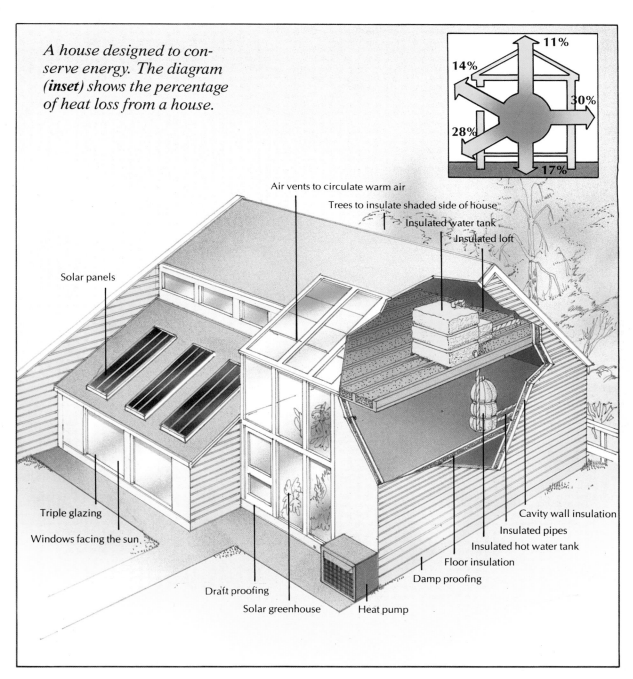

*A house designed to conserve energy. The diagram (**inset**) shows the percentage of heat loss from a house.*

11%

14%

30%

28%

17%

Air vents to circulate warm air

Trees to insulate shaded side of house

Insulated water tank

Insulated loft

Solar panels

Triple glazing

Windows facing the sun

Draft proofing

Solar greenhouse

Heat pump

Damp proofing

Floor insulation

Insulated hot water tank

Insulated pipes

Cavity wall insulation

# Automation in the home

Automatic machines are very common in today's homes. Some of them are very simple, such as alarm clocks and pop-up toasters. Others, such as microwave ovens, washing machines, and electronic sewing machines, can perform more complex tasks. Video recorders can turn themselves on and ignore commercials when they tape TV.

*Below   A modern electronic sewing machine can be programmed to produce a variety of stitches.*

*Above   A tumble drier is a very simple automatic machine; it just switches off after a preset time.*

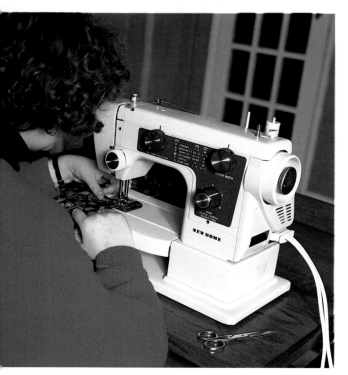

All automatic machines, however, are capable of exercising some form of self control. That means that part of the output (the work the machine does) is used to control what the machine does next. The simplest type of automatic machine is one that has some sort of feedback device for switching the machine off or on. For example, a refrigerator or a water heater has a temperature-sensitive switch known as a thermostat. Other machines may have electrically operated timers.

In addition, there may be mechanical or electrical switches that switch the machine from one type of an action to another. Early forms of the washing machine used such simple devices.

A modern washing machine, on the other hand, uses the electronic switches in a microprocessor, a simple form of computer. Machines controlled by microprocessors are now appearing in increasing numbers, and many people believe that homes of the future will be run by **robots**. A few very simple robots are already available, but these are really little more than toys for adults. Whether we will have real robots in the future seems doubtful. Everyday tasks like cleaning, ironing, and mowing the lawn may seem simple to us, but they actually require very complicated actions that will be very difficult to teach to robots. In addition, robots operate more efficiently in well-ordered places. We might have to reorganize our homes and our lives to suit our robots! It would seem that in the future, there will be a limit to the amount of automation that can successfully be brought into our homes.

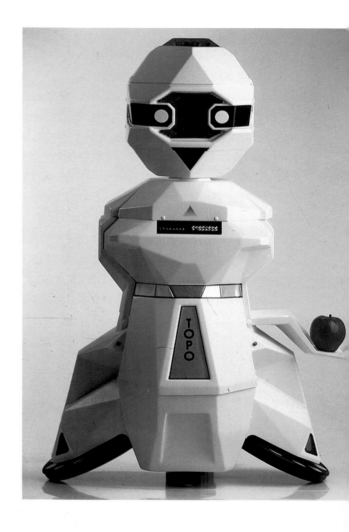

*Above*  TOPO is a simple domestic robot. It is operated via an infrared beam by a microcomputer. It can speak and move about, but like all existing domestic robots, its use is very limited.

19

# Computer control

We live in the age of the **microcomputer**, or desktop computer. But although microcomputers have a wide range of business uses, at present their use in the home is mostly limited to playing games. However, microcomputers are capable of much more than this. Already, there are devices—called **sensors**—that can link microcomputers to home lighting, plumbing, and security systems. The resulting computer network has the capacity to handle not only these large functions, but to control household appliances like the video recorder as well.

In the future, every home may have its own computer keeping a constant check on how everything is working. The home owner will just use a keyboard and a screen to see that everything is operating normally. The computer will be linked to sensors attached to the electrical wiring and plumbing and will give immediate warning of any fault. It will be left to the computer to decide which parts of the house to heat, according to the temperature outside and whether or not heat is needed. The computer could also be left to decide what fuel to use, depending on availability and cost. The computer will also be linked to the telephone, and, if necessary, it will send out emergency messages. The telephone link will also allow the house owner to contact the computer from any outside telephone, in order to receive information or give instructions.

*Left    The modern personal computer is the forerunner of the type that will control the home of the future.*

*Right    One day a computer will be the central controller of a completely integrated system in a home.*

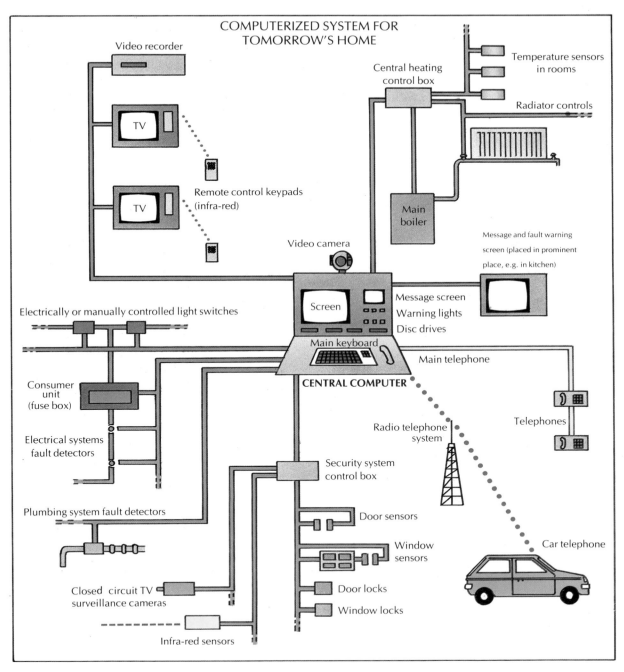

# COMPUTERIZED SYSTEM FOR TOMORROW'S HOME

Video recorder

Temperature sensors in rooms

Central heating control box

Radiator controls

TV

Remote control keypads (infra-red)

TV

Main boiler

Message and fault warning screen (placed in prominent place, e.g. in kitchen)

Video camera

Screen

Message screen

Electrically or manually controlled light switches

Warning lights

Disc drives

Main keyboard

Main telephone

CENTRAL COMPUTER

Consumer unit (fuse box)

Telephones

Radio telephone system

Electrical systems fault detectors

Security system control box

Plumbing system fault detectors

Door sensors

Window sensors

Car telephone

Closed circuit TV surveillance cameras

Door locks

Window locks

Infra-red sensors

# Home security

As people acquire an increasing number of valuable possessions that are easily stolen, home security is becoming more and more important. It is unfortunate, but it seems that homes of the future must be made very secure against entry by intruders.

Burglars can be physically prevented from entering houses. Doors and windows can be made secure with locks. At present such locks are mostly mechanical devices that need keys. But in the future locks may be electronically controlled. Such locks could be programmed to recognize cards which have been given a special magnetic pattern. If the "key" were lost or stolen, a door

*Above* Closed-circuit television may be used in our homes as a way of detecting intruders.

*Left* Modern security systems often use an infrared sensor to detect burglars.

22

lock could immediately be reprogrammed to recognize another magnetic pattern. Eventually, door locks may not need keys at all; in the future they will be able to recognize their owner's fingerprints or voices. The windows of a house could all be locked electronically in one step by a particular coded radio signal.

Another way of discouraging intruders is to install a system for detecting their presence and setting off an alarm. Future security systems will probably be linked to the house computer, which may also be able to monitor what is going on by means of **closed circuit television**. The computer will also be able to turn lights on and off while the owners are away, to fool burglars into thinking that someone is home.

*Below* A window contact switch is the eye and ear of a burglar alarm system.

# Communications

*Above* *A home computer can be used to communicate with other computers via the telephone network.*

*Left* *Using the home computer to select and pay for merchandise*

The most important systems of communication used in the home include the telephone and television. At present, most people use these separately. The television can be used for receiving computer-stored information via **teletext** services, and the telephone is generally used simply for speaking to other people.

However, the television and telephone can be linked together, as they are in **viewdata** information services. Viewdata information passes through telephone wires to appear on a television screen. At present, viewdata services are mostly used by businesses, but a revolution is taking place in communications. In the home of the future, the telephone and the television are likely to form part of a complete, integrated communications system, linked to the house computer.

*Right* *Satellite receivers allow viewers to watch television programs beamed from other parts of the world.*

Using this system, it will be possible to link up the house computer with any other computer, anywhere in the world. Everyone will be able to send **electronic mail** and leave advertisements and messages on electronic notice boards. In the same way, it will be possible for people to do most of their shopping without leaving home, simply by calling up a store's computer. They will be able to make a selection from the goods displayed on the screen. Payment for the goods will be transferred automatically. It will also be possible to use the system for handling financial affairs, such as paying bills and moving money between bank accounts. Schoolchildren will be able to use the system to help control their own educations, by contacting central computers for information or using educational computer programs.

# The portable office

Modern communications systems are already making it possible for people to work away from the office. In the future, it seems likely that more and more people will spend time working at home. People who need to travel will be able to do much of their work in hotels or in their car.

The key to the portable office is, of course, the microcomputer. Already there are many kinds that can be used to carry out a range of office tasks, such as accounting, stock keeping, storing and retrieving information, business planning, designing, drawing, and word processing. Computers can now be linked to one another by the telephone system, and this is likely to become much easier in the future. A future office might have a central computer linked to a number of outlying microcomputers in people's homes. Video telephones could also help people keep in touch with each other.

*Right   Using microcomputers linked to a central office computer, many people will be able to work at home.*

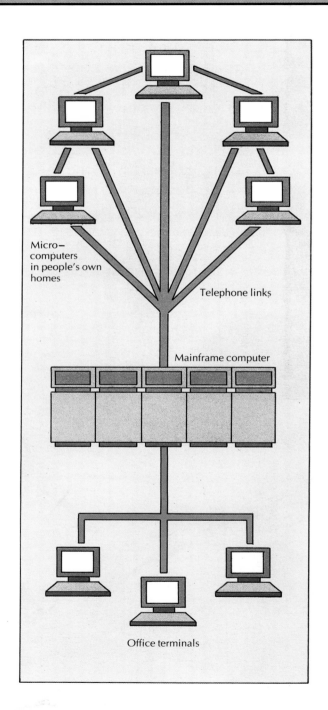

Micro–computers in people's own homes

Telephone links

Mainframe computer

Office terminals

Nor will out-of-office workers necessarily have to remain near their home computers. Already there are small, easily portable machines that can be used anywhere at all. When the user returns home, he or she can simply connect the portable computer to the home computer and transfer the new information automatically. Mobile telephones now enable people to contact anyone from wherever they happen to be. In the future, it should be possible to connect such telephones to portable computers, thus allowing people to send or receive information anywhere in the world.

*Above    Mobile telephones allow people to communicate wherever they are. Soon it should be possible to link such telephones to portable computers.*

*Right    The video telephone could make office communications easier by allowing people to see as well as speak to each other.*

# Leisure

It seems likely that people will have increasing amounts of leisure time in the future. Much of this time will probably be spent on traditional pastimes, such as reading books, working on hobbies, and traveling. But there will also be a much greater demand for home entertainment, and this demand will be met largely by the broadcasting and electronics industries.

Television will be much in demand. The number of available channels seems likely to increase and many people will be able to receive programs from the other side of the world, beamed in from **communications satellites**. Some programs will be supplied by cable television companies. And, if the cables have two-way links, it will be possible to allow viewers actually to take part in a variety of programs. Television sets, too, may change. Flat screen televisions that can hang on the wall like pictures are already being designed, and eventually there may be **three-dimensional** television.

Other kinds of home entertainment will include advanced computer

*Left*  A cable television studio is a complex place. Cable television signals travel along cables rather than on radio waves. Cable television companies aim to provide an alternative to traditional broadcasting companies and offer viewers the chance of actually playing a part in some programs.

games. Music will be played on complex equipment, and it will sound much clearer thanks to the superb sound quality possible from **compact discs** and digital audio tapes. Taped video may be replaced by **video discs**. Video discs make it possible for the viewer to influence the order in which the individual video frames are played and thus affect what happens.

With these scientific advances rapidly taking place in our homes, it would seem that the world of the future will be an exciting place in which to live.

***Above*** *A video disc can be used to store vast amounts of information in the form of pictures and sound.*

***Left*** *Many stereo systems now include a compact disc player as well as a conventional turntable, a radio tuner, and two tape players.*

# Glossary

**clinker** A hard material formed when coal ash is heated to such a high temperature that it melts and fuses together

**closed circuit television** A system in which signals are transmitted from camera to receiver, forming a closed circuit

**communications satellite** An artificial satellite used to send radio, television, and telephone signals around the earth's surface

**compact disc** A disc containing a sound recording made by using a laser to dig a pattern of "pits" which record electrical signals. The pits can be read by another laser on a compact disc player.

**computer** An electronic machine that can be programmed to carry out different tasks

**double glazing** A window having two sheets of glass (or transparent plastic) separated by an air gap

**electronic mail** A process in which documents, such as letters, are sent along telephone lines from one computer to another

**fossil fuel** Any natural fuel such as coal, oil, or gas that was originally formed underground from the compressed bodies and tissues of prehistoric animals and plants

**Industrial Revolution** A time in the eighteenth and nineteenth centuries when power-driven machines rapidly changed the world's economy

**microcomputer** A small, desktop computer, consisting of a keyboard, disc drive, and screen

**prefabricated** Partly built at a factory

**robot** A computer-controlled machine capable of carrying out a number of different tasks

**sensor** Sensitive equipment that responds to changes around it, such as a change in temperature

**silica** A name given to the chemical silicon dioxide, which occurs naturally as quartz and other rocks

**teletext** A computer system where information is broadcast over a television channel. Anyone with a receiver that can decode the signals can have the information displayed on his or her television screen.

**three-dimensional image** An image that has depth as well as width and height

**vermiculite** A mineral that can be made into a lightweight, water-absorbent material for insulation

**video disc** A disc containing a recording of sound and pictures made by using a laser to record electrical signals as a pattern of small digs or "pits." The pits can be read by another laser on a video disc player.

**viewdata** Information that is stored in a central computer and which can be sent along telephone lines and displayed on television

# Books to read

*Living with Tomorrow* by Richard M. Stephenson (John Wiley and Sons, 1981)

*Understanding Communications Systems* by Don L. Cannon, Ph.D (Texas Instruments, 1984)

*Living in the Future* by Mark Lambert (Wayland, 1985)

*Videotext* by Efrem Sigel (Harmony Books, 1980)

*The World of Tomorrow* by Robin Kerrod (Longman, 1980)

## Houses and Homes

Building Homes
Castles and Mansions
Homes in Cold Places
Homes in Hot Places

Homes in Space
Homes in the Future
Homes on Water
Mobile Homes

## Picture acknowledgements

The author and publishers would like to thank the following for allowing their illustrations to be reproduced in this book: Bryan and Cherry Alexander, p. 13 (bottom); Calyx Photo Library, p. 9 (top); Bruce Coleman, pp. 8 (top), 11 (bottom), 12; OXFAM, p.13 (top); PHOTRI, pp. 7 (top), 8 (bottom), 20, 23; The Research House, p. 5; Science Photo Library, *cover*; Sefton Photo Library, pp. 16 (both), 18 (both), 22 (bottom), 29 (bottom); Telefocus/British Telecommunications, pp. 22 (top), 24 (both), 25, 27 (both), 28; ZEFA Photo Library, pp. 4 (bottom), 7 (bottom), 10, 11 (top), 29 (top). All other pictures from the Wayland Picture Library.

# Index